Sustainable Futures

Sustainable Futures

A PRACTICAL GUIDE TO LIVING GREEN

Anurag Anurag

Anurag Anurag

Contents

1

The Case for Change: Embracing Sustainability in Everyday Life

Sustainability is more than just a buzzword; it's an essential approach to modern living. As we face critical environmental challenges such as climate change, pollution, and the depletion of natural resources, the need for each of us to consider the impact of our daily choices has never been more urgent. This book is designed to guide you through understanding, implementing, and benefiting from sustainable practices, with the ultimate aim of reducing your environmental footprint.

The concept of sustainability involves meeting our own needs without compromising the ability of future generations to meet theirs. It spans a broad spectrum of activities and choices, from conserving energy and minimizing waste to opting for renewable resources. This guide aims not only to educate but also to inspire actionable changes that lead to a healthier, more sustainable way of living.

Many people feel overwhelmed by the constant stream of alarming environmental news and are confused by the conflicting advice on how to effect meaningful personal and community change. This book aims to demystify the complexities of sustainable living by breaking them down into practical, manageable steps. Whether it's choosing eco-friendly fashion, reducing household waste, or understanding the ins and outs of renewable energy, this guide provides clear, concise, and actionable advice.

Our journey through the various aspects of sustainable living will show you that small changes, when multiplied by millions of people, can transform the world. You'll find that adopting sustainable practices not only contributes to the global effort to mitigate environmental degradation but also offers personal benefits, such as cost savings and a healthier lifestyle. This book is your first step towards a deeper understanding and a more proactive stance on environmental responsibility. By the end, you'll see that everyone has a part to play, and that your actions—no matter how small they may seem—can have a profound impact on our planet's future.

2

Understanding Your Carbon Footprint

Every choice we make has an environmental impact, often quantified as a 'carbon footprint.' This term measures the total greenhouse gases, primarily carbon dioxide, emitted by our actions, encompassing everything from household energy use to transportation, and even the lifecycle of the products we consume.

Gaining insight into your carbon footprint is crucial for adopting more sustainable practices. It involves a thorough assessment of personal and household energy consumption, travel habits, dietary choices, and overall consumption patterns. Tools and resources like online carbon calculators can help quantify these emissions, offering a clear picture of where reductions can be most effectively made.

By understanding and calculating our carbon footprint, we can see the direct effects of our lifestyle choices on the environment. This awareness allows us to identify significant areas for emission reduction, such as optimizing home energy use, choosing more sustainable travel options, adopting a lower-impact diet, and being more conscious of the products we buy and use.

Reducing our carbon footprint doesn't just benefit the planet; it often aligns with healthier, more economically savvy lifestyles. Simple actions, such as improving home insulation, switching to energy-efficient appliances, and reducing meat consumption, not only decrease emissions but can also lower utility bills and improve personal health.

Moreover, engaging in effective recycling, composting, and waste reduction further helps in decreasing the ecological impact. These efforts are complemented by water conservation measures like installing low-flow fixtures and using rainwater for gardening, which conserve vital resources and reduce reliance on municipal systems.

Transitioning to a sustainable lifestyle involves a commitment to continuous improvement and re-evaluation. As we implement changes and track their impact, it becomes easier to make further adjustments that help in living more harmoniously with our environment.

Understanding and mitigating your carbon footprint is an ongoing process that encourages a deeper connection with the natural world and promotes a sustainable future. It's about making conscious decisions that reflect our commitment to the planet's health and our own.

Continuously refining our approach to sustainability involves staying informed about new technologies and strategies that can further reduce our environmental impact. As advances in renewable energy, sustainable agriculture, and eco-friendly products develop, we have more opportunities to integrate these solutions into our daily lives.

An essential part of managing a carbon footprint is also participating in broader community and global efforts to promote sustainability. This can involve supporting policies that encourage environmental responsibility, engaging with community initiatives that focus on green living, and fostering an ethos of sustainability within local and wider circles.

The impact of individual actions is magnified when combined with collective efforts. By sharing knowledge, resources, and experiences, communities can significantly enhance their overall sustainability impact. Encouraging others to assess and reduce their carbon footprints can lead to a cumulative effect that substantially mitigates the overall environmental impact.

Furthermore, advocating for systemic change in corporate and governmental policies can drive broader environmental benefits. Supporting businesses that practice sustainability and pushing for government regulations that protect the environment are ways individuals can contribute beyond personal lifestyle choices.

In conclusion, understanding and reducing your carbon footprint is about much more than just tallying up emissions—it's about fostering a mindset of continuous improvement and proactive involvement in sustainable practices. It requires adaptability, persistence, and a commitment to integrating sustainability deeply into our lives and communities. By taking these steps, we not only help safeguard the planet but also enrich our lives with a deeper connection to the world around us.

3

Zero-Waste Living

Embracing a zero-waste lifestyle is about making choices that aim to eliminate waste altogether, not just recycle more. The zero-waste philosophy is underpinned by five key principles, commonly known as the 5 Rs: Refuse, Reduce, Reuse, Recycle, and Rot.

Refuse what you do not need. Begin by saying no to single-use plastics, junk mail, and any items that are destined for a short life before heading to landfill.

Reduce what you do need. Simplify your life by purchasing only essentials, buying in bulk to avoid packaging, and choosing high-quality items that last longer.

Reuse by finding a second life for items that might otherwise be thrown away. Shop for secondhand goods, repurpose containers, and repair items instead of discarding them.

Recycle what you cannot refuse, reduce, or reuse. Educate yourself about your local recycling program to ensure you're recycling correctly, and seek out recycling options for items your curbside program won't take.

Rot refers to composting organic waste. Composting kitchen scraps and yard waste can turn what would be methane-producing trash in a landfill into rich soil for your garden.

Embracing the principles of zero-waste requires integrating practical habits into your daily routine. A zero-waste kitchen is a foundational aspect, involving mindful grocery shopping and efficient food storage. By selecting bulk items and fresh produce without packaging, and utilizing reusable containers, you can significantly cut down on kitchen waste.

Food storage also plays a key role in reducing waste. Using glass jars, cloth bags, and other sustainable alternatives keeps food fresh longer and eliminates the need for disposable wraps and packaging.

In the bathroom, reducing waste can be achieved through DIY solutions. Homemade toiletries such as toothpaste and deodorant are not only eco-friendly but also free from the unnecessary packaging and harmful chemicals often found in commercial products. These simple concoctions use natural ingredients and can be stored in reusable containers, contributing to both a healthier lifestyle and a cleaner environment.

By adopting a zero-waste lifestyle, not only can you significantly reduce your environmental impact, but you can also discover a simpler, more intentional way of living.

Beyond the basics, zero-waste living also extends to the broader aspects of life, such as clothing and home decor. We will guide you on how to approach fashion with a zero-waste mindset, advocating for a minimalist wardrobe composed of versatile, well-made pieces. The art of 'mending' becomes not just a practical skill but a statement against the disposable culture. You'll learn techniques for repairing and upcycling clothes, as well as strategies for conscious consumerism, like supporting brands that prioritize sustainability in their manufacturing processes.

The concept of a circular economy is central to zero-waste living. This approach is about designing out waste and ensuring that products are made to be made again. We'll explore how you can participate in and support a circular economy through choices in your everyday life. This might involve engaging in community swap events, choosing refillable products, or even advocating for local policies that support zero-waste initiatives.

In addition to practices at home, it is better to maintain zero-waste habits while on the go. From bringing your own containers for take-out to carrying reusable water bottles and coffee cups, we provide advice on how to prepare for various scenarios. Dining out, traveling, and attending events can all be managed with minimal waste with the proper preparation and mindset.

The journey toward zero-waste living is as much about creativity and empowerment as it is about reducing waste. It's not a path of deprivation but one of innovation and fulfillment. Living without waste is about making respectful, informed choices for the environment that evolve with you over time. Every day offers new opportunities to learn and to enjoy the satisfaction that comes with making positive decisions.

Transitioning to zero-waste cooking begins with a mindful approach to grocery shopping. Opt for unpackaged, fresh produce and bulk items whenever possible, bringing your own reusable bags and containers. Embrace the whole vegetable by finding creative uses for parts typically discarded, such as beet greens or carrot tops. Broths can be easily made from vegetable scraps, and fruits nearing over-ripeness are perfect for smoothies or baking.

Meal planning is a cornerstone of zero-waste cooking. By organizing your meals for the week, you can avoid impulsive buys and ensure that you use ingredients efficiently. When it comes to food storage, swap out single-use plastics for glass or stainless-steel containers, beeswax wraps, and silicone lids.

For those with a garden, starting a compost bin is an excellent way to deal with organic waste. If you live in an apartment, vermicomposting, or worm composting, is a compact option that can turn your kitchen scraps into nutrient-rich compost.

Community engagement plays a vital role in the zero-waste movement. Participating in or starting a local composting program not only benefits the environment but also helps to build a sense of community. Sharing tools and appliances through a neighborhood library can greatly reduce the need for individual ownership, and attending a repair café can extend the life of your belongings.

When it comes to holidays and gift-giving, zero-waste living calls for creativity and thoughtfulness. Consider gifts of experiences, homemade goods, or items that encourage a sustainable lifestyle, such as a reusable coffee cup or a compost bin. Wrapping gifts in fabric or reused paper adds a personal touch without the waste.

Understanding and addressing skepticism from others is part of the process. Be prepared to share the reasons behind your lifestyle choice, focusing on the positive aspects like health benefits, cost savings, and the joy of a simpler life. Remember, your zero-waste journey can be a powerful testament to the viability and benefits of sustainable living.

Incorporating zero-waste principles does not have to strain your finances. In fact, by reducing consumption and repurposing materials, you can often save money. Be resourceful with what you have, repair instead of replace, and always consider the secondhand market before buying new.

In embracing a zero-waste lifestyle, every action counts. Whether you're perfecting your composting routine, volunteering in community sustainability efforts, or simply choosing to refuse a plastic straw, each decision contributes to a larger, collective effort to nurture and protect our environment.

The transition to a zero-waste lifestyle also invites exploration into the realm of natural home care. Creating your own cleaning products from simple ingredients like vinegar, baking soda, and essential oils can drastically reduce the number of chemicals in your home and the waste produced from purchasing multiple cleaning supplies. These natural alternatives are not only better for the environment but often more economical.

Another aspect to consider is the influence of technology in waste production. Reducing digital clutter by cleaning out old files and emails, unsubscribing from unnecessary digital subscriptions, and responsibly recycling electronic devices can mitigate the often-overlooked digital waste footprint.

It is also crucial to acknowledge the emotional aspect of zero-waste living. Letting go of items can be challenging, but the philosophy of zero waste encourages a reevaluation of what is truly needed and valuable. This process can lead to a more mindful and deliberate approach to consumption and possession, fostering a sense of clarity and purpose.

In conclusion, the shift to zero-waste living is a series of deliberate and thoughtful adjustments that collectively contribute to a larger environmental impact. It's about making informed choices that align with a commitment to sustainability. As this chapter demonstrates, adopting a zero-waste lifestyle is a transformative and continuous journey that not only benefits the planet but also enriches personal well-being.

4

Sustainable Fashion

The fashion industry stands as one of the significant contributors to environmental degradation, yet it also holds immense potential for positive change. Sustainable fashion is about more than just choosing eco-friendly fabrics; it encompasses a holistic approach to the clothes we wear, considering how they're made, who makes them, and the lifecycle they lead before and after they're in our wardrobe.

This shift begins with fabric selection. Natural, organic materials like organic cotton, hemp, and bamboo grow with less water and no pesticides, reducing their environmental impact. Meanwhile, recycled materials give a second life to what would otherwise be waste.

But sustainable fashion also delves into the ethics of clothing production. It's crucial to support brands and designers who ensure fair wages and safe working conditions for their workers. Transparency in the supply chain allows consumers to make informed choices that align with their values.

The concept of a 'capsule wardrobe' plays a significant role in sustainable fashion. It's about curating a selection of garments that are versatile, timeless, and long-lasting. This not only cuts down on consumption and waste but also encourages a more personal and creative approach to fashion.

Care and maintenance of clothing are also pivotal. Simple practices like washing clothes in cold water, air drying, and following proper care instructions can extend the life of garments and decrease energy and resource use. Additionally, learning basic repair skills can save a favorite piece from ending up in a landfill.

Sustainable fashion is not just about buying; it's about a shift in mindset. It involves embracing second-hand and vintage pieces, upcycling old clothes into new creations, and when necessary, recycling garments responsibly. Community initiatives like clothing swaps and lending libraries are innovative ways to keep fashion in circulation.

Engaging with sustainable fashion also means understanding the lifecycle of our garments. Each piece of clothing has a story, from the cultivation of its fibers to its eventual disposal. To reduce the environmental footprint, consider the end-of-life for each garment. Favor brands that offer recycling programs or repurpose materials, ensuring that when a piece of clothing is no longer wearable, it doesn't just become another piece of waste.

Another crucial aspect is the frequency of purchases. Fast fashion has led to a culture of disposable clothing, with trends changing rapidly and clothes being discarded just as quickly. Adopting a sustainable fashion approach often involves resisting the lure of fast fashion. Instead, it encourages investing in quality over quantity and valuing clothing as more than just a temporary commodity.

For those who love the creativity and newness that fashion can bring, sustainable fashion opens the door to innovative materials and methods. Designers across the globe are experimenting with fabrics made from food waste, like pineapple leather or mushroom fiber, and utilizing dyes made from natural, non-toxic sources. These advancements not only push the boundaries of fashion but also pave the way for a more sustainable industry.

The conversation around sustainable fashion also includes advocacy and education. By talking about the importance of sustainable practices, sharing resources, and supporting sustainable fashion movements, consumers can help shift industry standards and create a demand for ethical and environmentally friendly practices.

This chapter would not be complete without addressing the role of activism within the sustainable fashion movement. From supporting garment workers' rights to campaigning against polluting practices, activism empowers consumers to push for the change they wish to see in the industry.

Sustainable fashion is a movement towards accountability, quality, and mindfulness. It represents a collective step forward in redefining what fashion means in society. It's about style and substance, where the clothes we choose to wear reflect our commitment to preserving the world around us.

The sustainable fashion movement is intertwined with systemic changes within the fashion industry. Advocacy for reduced water usage, minimized chemical dyes, and lower carbon emissions is crucial for long-term impact. Such systemic shifts are complemented by the innovative efforts of tech startups that are creating sustainable fabrics and efficient manufacturing processes.

New technologies have enabled the recycling of garments into fresh textiles, reducing waste. Brands that adopt these practices not only lead the industry in sustainability but also offer consumers clothing options that are both eco-conscious and modern.

Digital platforms serve as pivotal arenas for promoting sustainable fashion. Social media, when leveraged for advocacy and education, can inspire a larger audience to embrace sustainable choices. Influencers who highlight eco-friendly fashion demonstrate that style and environmental responsibility can go hand in hand.

Transparency is another critical element, as it enables consumers to make informed choices. Brands that disclose their production processes and material sources allow individuals to support practices that align with their values. This transparency fosters trust and accountability, encouraging brands to uphold ethical and sustainable standards.

Moreover, the rise of sustainable fashion isn't just in manufacturing and material sourcing; it's also about changing the narrative around fashion consumption. It encourages a cultural shift from the 'buy and dispose' model to one of longevity and meaning. Each piece of clothing is seen not just as an article of fashion but as an embodiment of personal values and a statement about the kind of world the wearer wants to live in and leave behind.

As part of this cultural shift, the encouragement to participate in local and global sustainability efforts takes on a personal note. It's about joining a community that values craftsmanship, ethics, and the environment. In a world of sustainable fashion, every thread counts, every purchase is deliberate, and every wardrobe is a testament to the wearer's commitment to a healthier planet.

The ethos of sustainable fashion also embraces the concept of 'slow fashion'—a counter-movement to fast fashion. This approach emphasizes quality craftsmanship, timeless designs, and longer-lasting materials. It supports smaller production runs and local artisans, reducing transportation emissions and promoting local economies.

In addition, slow fashion encourages consumers to form a deeper connection with their garments. This might involve learning the stories behind their clothes, understanding the journey of each item, and even connecting with the creators. This sense of connection can transform the act of getting dressed into a more meaningful ritual.

Fashion education plays a pivotal role in sustainability, informing consumers about the environmental and social impacts of their wardrobe choices. Workshops, documentaries, and educational programs raise awareness and teach skills such as textile repair, upcycling, and garment care, empowering individuals to take active roles in the life cycles of their clothing.

Another crucial practice in sustainable fashion is the responsible disposal of garments. Recycling and donating clothes extends their life, reduces waste, and supports those in need. Programs that repurpose textiles into insulation or stuffing material show the potential for innovation in recycling.

Sustainable fashion calls for a collaborative effort where consumers, designers, and policymakers work together for a greener future. As consumers, we have the power to drive change with every purchase and care choice we make. Designers and brands look to us to lead the way, and as the demand for sustainable options grows, the industry will adapt.

Every step towards sustainable fashion is a step towards a more ethical and ecologically balanced world. The choices we make can weave a new narrative for the fashion industry, one where beauty, style, and sustainability are interlaced in every garment.

In the practice of sustainable fashion, the lifecycle of a garment is extended through repair, alteration, and care. Initiatives like repair workshops not only help to maintain the longevity of clothing but also revive the tradition of mending, reinforcing the bond between the wearer and their wardrobe. This reintroduction of traditional skills combats the throwaway culture and fosters a sense of pride in maintaining and cherishing clothing.

The conversation around sustainable fashion also includes a critical look at packaging and shipping. Eco-friendly packaging solutions are becoming more prevalent, with biodegradable and recycled materials replacing traditional plastic packaging. Combined with carbon-neutral shipping options, brands are finding ways to minimize their environmental footprint in the e-commerce era.

Within this landscape, the role of legislation becomes evident. Policies that encourage sustainable practices, such as extended producer responsibility (EPR) schemes, can promote industry-wide changes. Such regulations may require manufacturers to be accountable for the entire lifecycle of their products, including take-back, recycling, and disposal programs.

Sustainable fashion also opens the dialogue about the true cost of clothing. It advocates for pricing that reflects the environmental and social costs of production, nudging consumers to recognize the value of ethically made garments. This awareness can shift consumer habits towards investing in quality pieces that last longer, rather than succumbing to the constant churn of fast fashion trends.

Collectively, these efforts depict a multifaceted approach to sustainable fashion. It's an ongoing narrative that seeks to harmonize the aesthetics of fashion with the ethics of production and the principles of environmental stewardship. Each element—from the raw materials to the hands that craft the clothing, from the moment of purchase to the end of life— plays a part in shaping a more sustainable fashion industry.

As individuals navigate through this evolving space, the collective impact of their choices propels the industry towards a more sustainable and equitable future. Sustainable fashion is not just a fleeting trend but a comprehensive, collective movement toward a more thoughtful and conscientious way of expressing one's style.

In addition to the broader changes and individual habits, sustainable fashion often involves direct action and advocacy. This can range from supporting environmental campaigns that call for industry reforms to participating in clothing repair and upcycling events that promote hands-on sustainability. Through such activism, consumers become part of a larger narrative that demands change and accountability from fashion industry leaders.

Furthermore, there's an emerging trend of utilizing technology to enhance sustainable practices. Apps that track the sustainability of a brand, online platforms for swapping clothes, and digital tools for managing a capsule wardrobe are all part of this digital shift towards eco-friendly fashion.

Lastly, the role of collaboration in sustainable fashion cannot be overstated. When designers, manufacturers, NGOs, and consumers come together, the potential for innovation and transformation in the industry is immense. These partnerships can lead to breakthroughs in sustainable materials, ethical labor practices, and circular economies that redefine the future of fashion.

The essence of sustainable fashion is captured in the understanding that every choice we make, from the fabric we select to the care we give our clothes, contributes to a greener world. It is a movement that harnesses the expressive power of fashion not only to declare personal style but also to articulate our vision for the future.

As we draw this chapter to a close, it is with the recognition that readers are now armed with the knowledge to navigate their fashion journey consciously. They are aware of their fashion footprint and understand the significance of their choices. It is an invitation to step into the role of advocate, to actively shape a sustainable future in the world of fashion.

5

Green Building and Sustainable Home Management

The intersection of architecture and sustainability forms the core of green building—a practice that integrates environmental responsibility and resource efficiency into every stage of the building process. From design to demolition, green building focuses on reducing the environmental impact of homes while enhancing the health and comfort of those living within.

Sustainable home management complements green building by focusing on the operation and maintenance of the home. It involves using energy more efficiently, reducing waste, conserving water, and ensuring that the indoor environment is healthy.

One of the pillars of green building is energy efficiency. Homes designed or retrofitted with energy-saving features like double-glazed windows, proper insulation, and tight construction reduce the need for heating and cooling, leading to lower utility costs and a smaller carbon footprint.

Sustainable homes also incorporate renewable energy sources. Solar panels, for instance, can generate electricity and heat water, while geothermal systems can provide heating and cooling by harnessing the earth's stable temperatures. These technologies not only decrease dependence on fossil fuels but often come with financial incentives like tax credits and rebates.

Water conservation is another critical aspect. Installing low-flow faucets and toilets, harvesting rainwater for landscaping, and utilizing drought-resistant plants in the garden are all ways homeowners can manage water use more sustainably.

Materials used in green buildings are chosen for their durability, recyclability, and low environmental impact. Sustainable homes often feature materials like reclaimed wood, recycled metal, or rapidly renewable bamboo. Such choices not only add aesthetic value but also ensure that the house's environmental footprint is reduced.

Inside the home, sustainable management means choosing appliances and systems that conserve energy and water. Energy Star-rated appliances, LED lighting, and smart home technologies that optimize energy use can significantly impact a home's sustainability profile.

Proper waste management is a key component of a sustainable home. This includes composting organic waste, recycling as much as possible, and choosing products with minimal packaging.

A sustainable home is also a healthy home. This means using non-toxic paints, ensuring adequate ventilation to improve indoor air quality, and choosing furniture and fittings made from natural or non-toxic materials.

Living in a green building and managing a sustainable home is about making intentional choices that benefit the environment and the people living in it. It's about creating spaces that not only shelter but also nurture, conserve, and inspire.

To further the efforts of energy conservation, smart home technology plays an increasingly prominent role. Programmable thermostats, energy monitors, and intelligent lighting systems can be optimized to reduce consumption when a home is unoccupied, providing both comfort and efficiency.

The concept of green space within the home, such as indoor gardens and green walls, supports sustainable home management by improving air quality and providing a connection to nature. These living elements can enhance well-being and can even contribute to home food production, reducing the environmental cost associated with food transport.

When it comes to furnishings, sustainable home management advocates for furniture made from eco-friendly materials. It also encourages purchasing from local artisans and craftsmen, reducing the carbon footprint associated with long-distance transportation. Additionally, choosing furniture designed to last and that can be repaired or repurposed ensures longevity and reduces the need for frequent replacements.

Home management extends into the realm of cleaning and maintenance. Using natural cleaning products or homemade solutions can significantly reduce the presence of harmful chemicals in the home and their release into the environment. This approach safeguards the health of the household and the planet.

An essential part of sustainable home management is ongoing education and adaptation. As technology advances and new sustainable materials and methods become available, homeowners are encouraged to stay informed and consider upgrades or changes that could enhance their home's sustainability.

Furthermore, green building and sustainable home management are not exclusive to new constructions. Existing homes can be retrofitted with green technologies and sustainable practices. Simple measures, such as sealing drafts, adding insulation, or installing smart meters, can make a significant difference.

Energy and water audits are excellent tools for identifying areas where improvements can be made. These audits can be performed by professionals or through DIY kits and can help homeowners develop targeted strategies for increasing their home's efficiency.

Sustainable home management is a holistic approach to living that resonates with the ethos of environmental stewardship. It encompasses the daily operations of a home, the conscious decisions by the occupants, and the broader impact those decisions have on the world. Through mindful management and green building practices, homes can become havens of sustainability that contribute positively to the environment and offer a blueprint for a sustainable future.

Incorporating sustainable practices extends beyond the structure and systems of a home to the very behaviors and lifestyles of its inhabitants. Effective home management means regular reviews and updates of household routines to minimize energy and water usage. This might involve simple habits like turning off lights when leaving a room, taking shorter showers, and only running dishwashers and washing machines with full loads.

The principles of permaculture can also be applied to create sustainable landscapes that work in harmony with natural ecosystems. Designing a garden with native plants, for example, can support local wildlife, reduce water usage, and lower maintenance needs. Rain gardens and permeable paving also contribute to a property's sustainability by reducing runoff and recharging groundwater.

For urban dwellers, sustainable home management may mean participating in community energy programs or investing in shared renewable energy projects when individual installations aren't feasible. It also includes supporting local initiatives aimed at improving urban sustainability, such as tree-planting drives and community gardens.

The integration of green technology and sustainable practices into home management has the added benefit of potentially increasing property values. Green-certified homes can attract buyers interested in lower utility costs and environmental impact, proving that sustainability is not only good for the planet but can also be a wise economic decision.

Sustainability in the home also fosters a sense of connection and responsibility towards the community and the environment. It encourages the sharing of resources, such as tool libraries and neighborhood composting programs, which can reduce overall consumption and foster community ties.

In aiming for a sustainable home, it's essential to recognize that perfection is not the goal—progress is. Every step towards greener building and more responsible home management is a step in the right direction, contributing to a collective effort to mitigate environmental impacts.

The principles laid out in this section offer a roadmap for homeowners and renters alike to navigate the transition to more sustainable living spaces. These practices showcase that everyone has the potential to contribute to the sustainability movement, transforming individual actions into a collective force for global change.

Sustainable home management also embraces the concept of minimalism, which can lead to a reduction in overall consumption and waste. By focusing on what is truly essential and finding value in less, homeowners can decrease their environmental footprint. This minimalist approach is about quality over quantity, emphasizing the functionality and sustainability of possessions rather than excess.

Furthermore, sustainable homes often utilize innovative waste management strategies such as home-scale anaerobic digesters for organic waste, which not only reduce landfill contribution but can also provide biogas for cooking. Rigorous sorting systems for recyclables and education on proper disposal methods ensure that waste is handled responsibly.

The integration of home automation systems can also advance sustainability goals. These systems can manage resources more effectively by adjusting heating, cooling, and lighting based on usage patterns, presence detection, and even weather forecasting, ensuring optimal energy use and reducing waste.

Building a sustainable home is also about resilience and preparing for future environmental conditions. This includes considering climate change adaptability in home design, such as utilizing landscaping to protect against soil erosion or installing features that help manage extreme weather conditions.

In the broader scope of sustainability, the chapter highlights the importance of community action and policy advocacy. Homeowners can support or initiate local policies that encourage green building standards, energy efficiency incentives, and sustainable community development projects.

The narrative of a sustainable home is ever-evolving. As new technologies emerge and our understanding of ecological impact deepens, homeowners are encouraged to remain flexible and responsive. Education, community engagement, and a willingness to adopt new practices are the cornerstones of progressive sustainable home management.

Every action taken towards a greener home sends ripples through the fabric of society, influencing markets, policies, and cultural norms. It's in these everyday choices that we find the power to shape a sustainable living environment, one that honors the delicate balance of nature and seeks to preserve it for generations to come.

A sustainable home offers a blueprint for the future, demonstrating that our living spaces can be in harmony with nature, conserve resources, and support a healthier lifestyle. It is a holistic approach that balances environmental care, economic practicality, and social responsibility.

Through the adoption of energy-efficient systems, renewable energy, water-saving techniques, and waste reduction practices, homeowners can transform their spaces into models of sustainability. Such homes not only reduce carbon footprints and utility bills but also create nurturing environments that promote well-being.

The message is clear: building sustainably and managing homes with an eye toward conservation is not just beneficial—it's imperative for a thriving planet. These practices are steps toward a vision of living where every home is a pillar of sustainability, every action a commitment to preservation, and every individual a custodian of the world's future.

6

Renewable Energy Solutions

The transition to renewable energy is a cornerstone of global efforts to combat climate change and reduce our reliance on finite, polluting fossil fuels. This chapter explores the various renewable energy solutions that individuals and communities can adopt to power their lives sustainably.

Solar energy is one of the most accessible and widely used forms of renewable energy. With the installation of solar panels on rooftops, homeowners can harness the power of the sun to generate electricity for their daily needs. The technology has become more affordable and efficient, making it a practical choice for a wide range of climates and locations.

Wind energy, generated by wind turbines, is another viable option, particularly in areas with consistent wind patterns. While large-scale wind farms are common, small-scale turbines can also be installed on private property, offering another avenue for households to contribute to the green energy grid.

Geothermal energy taps into the earth's natural heat. Geothermal heat pumps can heat and cool homes by exploiting the constant temperatures just below the earth's surface. This method is incredibly efficient and can be implemented almost anywhere in the world.

Hydroelectric power, generated by capturing the energy of flowing water, is traditionally harnessed through large dams. However, newer technologies such as micro-hydro generators have made it possible for smaller streams and rivers to contribute to renewable energy production without the environmental disruption caused by large-scale projects.

The chapter also discusses the potential of emerging renewable technologies such as tidal and wave energy, which capture the energy of ocean currents and waves. While these technologies are still in the developmental stage, they represent the forward edge of renewable innovation.

Biomass energy, derived from organic materials like plant waste and manure, can be converted into electricity, heat, or biofuels. Although it is a form of renewable energy, its sustainability is dependent on careful management to ensure that biomass production does not compete with food sources or lead to deforestation.

Energy storage solutions are critical to the effectiveness of renewable energy. Battery systems, like home energy storage units, allow for the storage of excess power for use when the sun isn't shining or the wind isn't blowing. Advances in battery technology continue to improve the efficiency and capacity of these storage solutions.

Community-based renewable energy projects are also a key focus, enabling neighborhoods and cities to invest collectively in renewable installations. These projects not only provide clean power but also strengthen community bonds and support local economies.

Renewable energy solutions not only lessen environmental impact but can also offer financial benefits. Many regions offer incentives such as tax credits, rebates, or feed-in tariffs for those who invest in renewable energy systems.

Adoption of renewable energy is not only a technical change but also a cultural shift towards greater environmental consciousness. It requires individuals to become proactive about where their energy comes from and the long-term impact of their consumption choices.

The democratization of energy through renewables is empowering. Homeowners can now become part producers of their electricity, contributing excess power back to the grid. This not only creates a more distributed and resilient energy network but also allows individuals to play an active role in the energy economy.

The integration of smart grids is another facet of renewable energy solutions. These advanced electrical grids use digital communication technology to detect and react to local changes in usage. Smart grids support the dynamic balancing of supply and demand, accommodate the intermittent nature of renewable energy, and enhance the efficiency and stability of electricity distribution.

Renewable energy is also playing a crucial role in reducing energy poverty and boosting development in rural and remote areas. Off-grid solar and wind systems bring power to regions without access to a traditional grid, enabling communities to leapfrog into a new era of energy use that is clean and sustainable.

Education and awareness are essential in accelerating the shift to renewable energy. By providing clear information about the benefits and practicalities of renewables, as well as guidance on navigating the often complex landscape of incentives and regulations, communities can be mobilized to take collective action towards a renewable future.

Innovation and investment in renewable technologies are critical for advancing the capabilities and reach of sustainable energy solutions. Ongoing research and development are necessary to address current challenges and enhance the efficiency and integration of renewables into the energy market. Breakthroughs in technology, along with strategic changes in policy, financing, and business models, are essential for making renewable energy more accessible and practical for widespread adoption.

In discussing the holistic benefits of renewable energy, the chapter acknowledges the interconnectedness of energy use with broader environmental and social issues. Renewable energy can lead to healthier air quality, preservation of ecosystems, and a reduction in the harmful impacts of climate change.

Understanding and harnessing renewable energy extends beyond individual installations, involving a collective push towards a cleaner energy economy. With the growing urgency of climate change, the shift towards renewables also intersects with global efforts to lower carbon emissions and transition towards low-impact living.

The relationship between renewable energy and community development is profound. By engaging in community solar projects or wind cooperatives, communities not only share the costs and benefits of renewable energy but also strengthen their collective commitment to sustainable practices.

Advancements in renewable energy also support a transition to electric transportation, further reducing reliance on fossil fuels. The expansion of electric vehicles (EVs) and the accompanying infrastructure, such as charging stations powered by renewables, exemplify how the energy and transportation sectors can synergize to lower emissions.

Adopting renewable energy is also about embracing adaptability and resilience. As weather patterns become more unpredictable due to climate change, renewables offer a way to maintain stable energy supplies. Decentralized energy systems, like microgrids powered by local renewable sources, enhance a community's resilience against disruptions.

The role of policy cannot be understated in fostering a renewable energy future. Incentives and regulations that encourage the adoption of renewables, energy efficiency, and conservation are pivotal in steering both the public and private sectors towards sustainable energy practices.

As renewable technologies become more integrated into everyday life, they pave the way for new forms of energy literacy and engagement. From households to schools to businesses, the understanding of energy generation and consumption takes on a new significance, promoting a culture of sustainability.

The narrative of renewable energy is one of possibility and promise—a promise for a cleaner environment, a stable climate, and a sustainable energy supply that can meet the needs of the present without compromising the ability of future generations to meet their own.

The embrace of renewable energy is also a testament to human ingenuity and our ability to live in harmony with nature. The growing presence of solar arrays, wind turbines, and other renewable installations in landscapes around the world is a visible sign of this shift. They stand not just as mechanisms for power generation, but as symbols of a collective commitment to stewardship of the planet.

With the increasing feasibility of renewables, individuals are discovering new ways to participate in the energy transition. From installing solar panels on homes to investing in community renewable projects, there are diverse opportunities for contributing to a greener grid.

The financial sector has taken note of this paradigm shift, offering green bonds and other financial instruments to fund renewable projects. These initiatives demonstrate the potential for profitable investment that also yields environmental benefits.

Sustainability in energy also connects deeply with other areas of sustainability, such as water conservation and waste reduction. For example, the heat byproduct from solar panels can be used to warm water, and the use of organic waste can contribute to bioenergy production, showcasing the interconnected nature of sustainable systems.

Education initiatives and public outreach about renewables are fostering a new generation that values sustainability and is equipped with the knowledge to innovate further. Schools integrating solar panels not only reduce their carbon footprint but also serve as living labs where students can learn about clean energy firsthand.

Renewable energy solutions, therefore, represent a convergence of ethical, environmental, and practical considerations, each reinforcing the other. As society continues to innovate and invest in these technologies, we are building a legacy of a cleaner, more resilient, and equitable world.

As this discussion concludes, it is with the understanding that the journey toward renewable energy is continuous. It invites ongoing participation, learning, and adaptation, but most importantly, it calls for a collective vision and action to shape a sustainable future powered by the forces of nature.

7

Sustainable Transportation

Transportation is a critical component of our daily lives, yet it is also a significant source of greenhouse gas emissions worldwide. Sustainable transportation seeks to address this by promoting travel methods that minimize environmental impact, improve public health, and offer equitable access.

One of the most straightforward paths to sustainable transportation is through the use of public transit. Buses, trains, trams, and subways provide efficient travel for large numbers of people, reducing the per-person emissions compared to private vehicle use. Cities that invest in reliable and extensive public transit systems make sustainable travel accessible and convenient for their residents.

Active transportation, such as walking and cycling, not only reduces emissions but also contributes to physical health and well-being. Cities that offer safe and continuous pedestrian and bicycle infrastructure support these eco-friendly travel modes. The integration of bike-share programs and pedestrian-friendly urban design encourages a shift from car-centric to human-centric urban environments.

Electric vehicles (EVs) represent a significant shift in sustainable personal transportation. As battery technology advances and charging infrastructure expands, EVs offer a cleaner alternative to traditional gasoline-powered vehicles, particularly when paired with renewable energy sources.

Carpooling and ridesharing services are additional strategies that reduce the number of vehicles on the road, lowering traffic congestion and emissions. These communal travel options optimize the use of personal vehicles and provide flexible transportation alternatives without the need for car ownership.

For longer distances, high-speed rail and other mass transit options can provide sustainable alternatives to air travel, which is one of the most carbon-intensive travel methods. These high-speed trains are not only faster than car travel but also significantly more energy-efficient.

In the realm of freight and logistics, sustainable transportation involves optimizing delivery routes to reduce mileage and implementing practices like platooning, where trucks travel in a line to reduce air resistance and save fuel. The shift towards electric and hybrid delivery vehicles also plays a role in reducing emissions from goods transportation.

Urban planning and policy play crucial roles in promoting sustainable transportation. Policies that prioritize green transport infrastructure, incentivize EV purchases, and discourage unnecessary car use can shift the collective approach to how we travel.

Sustainable transportation is recognized not only as an environmental imperative but also as a catalyst for innovation and economic development. By embracing cleaner transport methods, societies can progress towards a future that is more sustainable, efficient, and interconnected.

Incorporating sustainable practices in transportation also involves a shift in personal mindset and public habits. The rise of telecommuting and remote work arrangements can significantly reduce the necessity for daily commutes, thus decreasing transportation emissions. As workplaces become more flexible, the traditional rush hour can be alleviated, leading to less congestion and a smaller carbon footprint from transport.

The potential of technology to enhance sustainable transportation is immense. Developments in intelligent transportation systems use data and connectivity to improve traffic flow, optimize route planning, and enhance the efficiency of public transport networks. Such systems can guide travelers to make smarter choices, such as traveling outside of peak times or choosing less congested routes.

For maritime and aviation sectors, the challenge is greater due to the heavy reliance on fossil fuels. However, advances in biofuels, along with increased efficiency in vessel and aircraft design, hold promise for reducing the environmental impact of these essential modes of long-distance transport.

The concept of green mobility extends beyond the vehicles and into the infrastructure they use. Green streets, for example, incorporate space for cyclists and pedestrians while managing stormwater and reducing urban heat through vegetation. Similarly, the development of EV charging stations using solar power can turn parking areas into clean energy hubs.

At the community level, local governments are increasingly recognizing the value of sustainable transport in urban planning. Initiatives to create car-free zones, develop extensive bike path networks, and improve pedestrian access not only support sustainability but also enhance the livability of cities.

Sustainable transportation also includes international and regional efforts to reduce emissions and improve efficiency. Agreements like the Paris Accord inspire countries to set ambitious targets for the reduction of transport emissions and to invest in the infrastructure and technology needed to meet those goals.

Moreover, the growth of the sharing economy has led to a reevaluation of the need for personal vehicle ownership. Car-sharing services and bike-sharing programs promote the idea that access to transportation can be just as convenient as ownership, without the associated costs and environmental impacts.

As sustainable transportation becomes increasingly integrated into the fabric of daily life, it brings with it a multitude of benefits: cleaner air, reduced noise pollution, and the preservation of the natural environment. This movement toward sustainable transport is an essential part of the journey towards a greener, more equitable world.

The role of education in sustainable transportation is paramount. Awareness campaigns and educational programs can inform the public about the benefits of sustainable transport and how to effectively utilize it. Schools incorporating bike-to-school programs or public transit training equip the next generation with the knowledge to make environmentally friendly travel choices.

Furthermore, the promotion of eco-friendly tourism practices encourages travelers to consider the environmental impact of their journeys. By opting for travel options with lower carbon footprints, such as trains over airplanes or bike tours instead of car rentals, tourists can enjoy their experiences responsibly.

Financial incentives also play a significant role in encouraging the adoption of sustainable transportation. Tax benefits, subsidies for electric vehicle purchases, toll exemptions for low-emission vehicles, and high-occupancy vehicle lanes are just some of the ways policymakers can make sustainable travel more attractive to the masses.

Sustainable transportation isn't just about the mode of travel; it's also about the distance traveled and the necessity of the trip. Urban design that promotes mixed-use developments can reduce the need for travel by placing homes, offices, shops, and entertainment within close proximity or even walking distance.

Lastly, sustainable transportation is about inclusivity and accessibility. Ensuring that all members of society have access to clean and efficient transport options is crucial. This includes addressing the mobility needs of the elderly, people with disabilities, and those living in underserved communities.

As we continue to innovate and push the boundaries of what is possible, the vision for sustainable transportation becomes clearer. It is a vision of a world where the journey is as important as the destination, and where the means of getting there is aligned with the health of our planet and its inhabitants.

The evolution of sustainable transportation is increasingly linked to the integration of technology and data analytics. With real-time tracking and mobile applications, public transit systems can provide up-to-the-minute updates, making them more user-friendly and efficient. This level of connectivity not only improves the user experience but also streamlines operations, reducing energy use and operational costs.

Electric and hybrid vehicles are becoming more sophisticated, with longer ranges and shorter charging times, making them a practical option for an increasing number of people. The expansion of charging infrastructure, including fast-charging stations along major highways and in urban centers, is essential to support the growing electric vehicle market.

In addition to technological advances, the success of sustainable transportation hinges on behavioral changes. Initiatives like "bike-to-work" days, rewards programs for public transit users, and educational campaigns about carpooling benefits can foster a culture where choosing sustainable transport options becomes the norm.

The transportation sector is also exploring the use of hydrogen fuel cells as a clean energy source. Vehicles powered by hydrogen emit only water vapor and can be refueled just as quickly as conventional cars, providing a promising alternative for reducing emissions from transportation.

Advocacy plays a crucial role in advancing sustainable transportation. Activists and non-profit organizations can effect change by lobbying for improvements in public transit, safer cycling and walking conditions, and policies that prioritize green transportation options.

The culmination of these efforts marks a significant shift towards a more resilient and adaptable transportation system. Sustainable transportation not only contributes to the mitigation of climate change but also represents a commitment to creating more livable cities and communities.

As this movement progresses, it is evident that the path towards sustainable transportation is not a solitary one. It is a collective journey that requires collaboration across sectors, disciplines, and borders. It is a journey that calls for the commitment of every individual, every community, and every nation to prioritize the health of the planet and the well-being of future generations.

Looking ahead, the landscape of sustainable transportation is poised to embrace further innovation, such as autonomous vehicles, which promise to optimize route efficiency and reduce traffic congestion. In conjunction, urban air mobility solutions, like drones and air taxis, open up the possibility of reducing ground traffic and associated emissions.

The impact of these advancements extends to the planning of cities and communities. Urban development can be reimagined with reduced need for parking spaces, giving way to more green spaces and pedestrian areas. This reclamation of space contributes to urban ecosystems, reduces heat island effects, and enhances the quality of life for city dwellers.

Collaboration between urban planners, technologists, environmental scientists, and the community is key to creating integrated transportation systems that are truly sustainable. The goal is a seamless mobility ecosystem where different modes of transportation work together efficiently and sustainably.

In rural areas, the challenge of sustainable transportation can be distinct. Here, the focus may be on improving the connectivity and efficiency of existing transportation, integrating ride-sharing models, and ensuring that clean transportation options are available and affordable.

Sustainable transportation also looks to the seas, advocating for cleaner shipping practices. Innovations such as wind-assisted propulsion and electric ferries offer the potential to reduce emissions from maritime transport, vital for the global trade system.

As we journey through the narrative of sustainable transportation, we recognize the profound potential of these solutions to revolutionize our world. They offer a chance to not only preserve the environment but to reinvent our very notion of mobility. This transformation, while complex, is essential for establishing a sustainable legacy that will propel humanity towards a more efficient and eco-conscious future.

The momentum is building, and with each step forward, sustainable transportation becomes more ingrained in the societal consciousness. It is a path marked by both challenge and opportunity, but most importantly, it is a path that leads to a cleaner, greener planet for all.

As we move further into the era of sustainable transportation, the emphasis on community-level initiatives becomes increasingly significant. Localized efforts such as community car-sharing programs and the promotion of 'complete streets'—which support safe travel for all users— show how tailored solutions can address specific needs while contributing to the larger goal of sustainability.

In addition to land and sea, the push for sustainable practices is reaching into the sky. Efforts to reduce the carbon footprint of air travel include the development of more fuel-efficient aircraft, the use of sustainable aviation fuels, and research into electric propulsion systems.

Equally important is the focus on equity and justice within sustainable transportation. Ensuring that all communities have equal access to clean and efficient transport options is critical for addressing social and environmental inequalities. This means not only providing affordable options but also ensuring that the benefits of clean transportation—such as improved air quality—are shared by all.

The convergence of sustainability with digital innovation offers smart solutions such as integrated mobility apps that combine public transport, ride-sharing, and bike rentals into a single, user-friendly interface. These digital platforms can simplify sustainable travel, making it a more attractive choice for daily commuters.

Education and community engagement remain pivotal, helping to instill a mindset where sustainable transportation is valued and pursued. Outreach programs in schools, workplaces, and neighborhoods can spread knowledge about the benefits of sustainable transport and the role individuals can play in reducing their transportation footprint.

As sustainable transportation evolves, it's increasingly clear that it's not just about changing how we travel—it's about transforming our relationship with the environment and each other. It's about creating a system that supports not just mobility but also health, community, and ecological balance.

The story of sustainable transportation is ongoing, and each advancement, each policy change, and each individual choice writes a new chapter in this evolving tale. It is a narrative of progress, one where every step toward sustainable mobility contributes to a larger journey of environmental and social harmony.

The drive towards sustainable transportation is a multifaceted endeavor, underpinned by the collective desire for a cleaner, more equitable world. Through a combination of technological innovation, policy reform, community action, and individual responsibility, we are witnessing a pivotal transition in how we move and connect.

This shift not only represents an evolution in the mechanics of travel but also embodies a broader commitment to environmental stewardship and social well-being. As sustainable transportation becomes more integrated into the fabric of society, it paves the way for communities that are not only more connected but also more attuned to the natural world.

Concluding this narrative, sustainable transportation emerges as a key component of a resilient future. It is a testament to the potential for harmony between human progress and ecological preservation. By reimagining mobility, we are not just traversing physical distances but bridging the gap to a sustainable future.

8

❧

Responsible Consumption and Recycling

Responsible consumption and recycling hinge on the commitment to making sustainable choices and minimizing waste. Embracing the 'reduce, reuse, and recycle' mantra involves purchasing fewer and more durable goods, thus challenging the throwaway culture that's prevalent today. This sustainable approach extends product lifespans, conserves resources, and cuts down on waste.

Reusing items not only diverts waste from landfills but also sparks creativity and innovation. Whether it's repurposing containers for new uses or upcycling clothes into new fashion statements, reuse can reduce the demand for new resources and breathe new life into old items.

Recycling is a critical process that transforms discarded materials into valuable resources again. Effective recycling reduces the reliance on raw material extraction, conserves energy, and cuts greenhouse gas emissions. Understanding how to recycle correctly—cleaning items, avoiding wishful recycling, and adhering to local guidelines—is key to reducing contamination and enhancing the efficacy of recycling programs.

Making informed choices about consumption means supporting businesses that adopt transparent and sustainable practices. Learning about various labels and certifications enables consumers to choose products that align with their values, fostering a market that values sustainability.

Electronics should be disposed of responsibly, considering the proper recycling channels to recover valuable materials and prevent environmental contamination. With e-waste on the rise, it's important to support and utilize certified e-waste recycling facilities.

Managing food waste is also critical. Home composting or contributing to community compost can convert organic waste into nutrient-rich soil, mitigating the impact of methane emissions from landfills and returning valuable nutrients to the earth.

The pursuit of responsible consumption and recycling also involves advocating for products designed with their end-of-life in mind. Encouraging manufacturers to create products that are easier to repair, upgrade, or recycle is part of a broader push toward a circular economy, where products and materials are kept in use for as long as possible.

By prioritizing these sustainable practices, individuals can significantly impact the health of the environment, paving the way for a future where resources are valued and conserved for generations to come.

The principles of responsible consumption and recycling encourage a departure from disposability and a move towards mindful stewardship of resources. This philosophy is reinforced by choosing to support companies that use environmentally friendly packaging or offer take-back programs for their products, ensuring that the materials can be reused or recycled at the end of their life cycle.

Additionally, reducing single-use plastics by opting for alternatives like biodegradables or refillable containers can drastically cut down on plastic waste, a major environmental pollutant. Investment in reusable items such as water bottles, shopping bags, and lunch containers can make a significant dent in the amount of waste generated daily.

For items that do reach the end of their usability, recycling plays a vital role in resource management. Educating oneself about the nuances of local recycling—what can and cannot be recycled, the need to sort, and how materials should be prepared for recycling—is crucial for making sure recyclable materials don't end up in a landfill.

In the larger context, responsible consumption involves community engagement and collective action. Participating in local waste reduction initiatives, community clean-ups, and educational workshops can amplify the impact of individual actions.

As we consider the lifecycle of products, it becomes clear that recycling is just one part of a larger system. Engaging in the circular economy requires not only recycling but also considering how products are made and what happens to them after use. This can include renting or borrowing items instead of owning, repairing instead of replacing, and ultimately choosing to invest in items designed with their entire lifecycle in mind.

Ultimately, responsible consumption and recycling are about fostering a culture of care—care for the products we use, the people who make them, and the world that provides the resources. It is about making choices that ensure the well-being of the environment and society, reflecting a deep understanding of and commitment to sustainability.

This culture of care extends to how communities deal with larger items and electronics that become obsolete. Repair cafes and tech refurbishment centers are on the rise, serving as hubs where items are given a second chance rather than being discarded. These community initiatives not only reduce waste but also teach valuable skills, strengthen community bonds, and promote a more sustainable economy.

When it comes to food consumption, a similar ethic applies. Choosing locally sourced and seasonal foods reduces the carbon footprint associated with long-distance transport. Moreover, understanding and practicing the principles of a sustainable diet, which emphasizes plant-based choices and reduces meat consumption, can have profound effects on personal health and the environment.

Water usage is another area where responsible consumption is key. Simple measures like fixing leaks, installing water-efficient fixtures, and using water-wise gardening techniques contribute significantly to conserving this precious resource.

Beyond individual and community actions, there is a role for policy and infrastructure to support responsible consumption and recycling. Encouraging developments include the creation of more comprehensive recycling facilities, clearer labeling of recyclable materials, and government incentives that encourage sustainable practices.

In fostering a sustainable future, education remains paramount. Schools and educational institutions play a vital role in cultivating an understanding of the environment and our impact on it. Integrating sustainability into curricula and promoting hands-on learning experiences can empower the next generation to be conscientious stewards of the planet.

Each act of responsible consumption and each effort to recycle is a step toward reducing our ecological footprint. By living more mindfully and consuming more consciously, we can ensure that our daily habits contribute to a more sustainable and equitable world.

The momentum behind responsible consumption and recycling is also driving innovation in waste management technology. Innovations like advanced sorting systems, which can more accurately separate recyclables, and new recycling technologies that can process previously non-recyclable materials, are enhancing our ability to reclaim and reuse.

In urban settings, 'zero waste' programs aim to eliminate all discharges to land, water, or air that may be a threat to planetary, human, animal, or plant health. Cities around the world are adopting zero waste goals, implementing strategies that encourage reduction, reuse, and recycling throughout communities.

Corporate responsibility plays a critical role as well. More companies are adopting sustainable practices, from reducing packaging to taking back products at the end of their lifecycle for recycling or proper disposal. The rise of product-service systems—where companies retain ownership of the product and provide it as a service—also reflects a shift toward circular business models.

Moreover, the push for responsible consumption and recycling isn't just limited to waste—it also includes energy use. Energy-efficient products, from LED light bulbs to high-efficiency appliances, contribute to the overall reduction of an individual's or household's energy footprint.

The adoption of responsible consumption and recycling practices is indicative of a larger cultural shift towards valuing sustainability and recognizing the finite nature of our resources. As more individuals embrace these practices, a collective force for change emerges, capable of driving significant environmental improvements.

The narrative of responsibility in consumption is ongoing and evolving. It is shaped by each person who chooses to live sustainably, each community that supports recycling, and each business that commits to eco-friendly practices. Together, these efforts construct a vision of a world where resources are respected, conservation is ingrained, and sustainability is a shared responsibility

As the journey towards comprehensive recycling and responsible consumption progresses, the concept of 'upcycling'—transforming by-products, waste materials, or unwanted products into new materials or products of better quality—gains traction. This creative take on reuse not only reduces waste but also adds value, showcasing the potential for a regenerative approach to our resources.

Financial systems are responding to this shift as well, with the emergence of green financing and investment in sustainability-focused initiatives. Whether funding the development of new recycling technologies or backing companies with strong sustainability credentials, the financial sector's engagement is a powerful driver for scaling up responsible consumption and recycling.

The shift to responsible consumption also asks for a broader understanding of global supply chains. Consumers are increasingly seeking transparency, wishing to understand the lifecycle of products—from raw material extraction to manufacturing and distribution. This awareness can influence purchasing decisions, steering the market toward more sustainable options.

Furthermore, the principles of responsible consumption are being woven into the fabric of communities through local sustainability programs, which often include educational components about waste and resource use. These programs provide the tools and knowledge necessary for individuals to make informed decisions that align with sustainability goals.

The collective impact of individual actions, when coupled with community initiatives and corporate responsibility, can lead to substantial environmental progress. It's a reinforcing cycle: as more people demand sustainable products and practices, more businesses will adopt them, which in turn makes it easier for individuals to consume responsibly.

In closing, the embrace of responsible consumption and recycling is about much more than just waste—it's about rethinking our relationship with the material world. It's about recognizing that each item we use and each decision we make has far-reaching implications for the environment and for future generations. By choosing to consume responsibly and recycle diligently, we actively participate in the creation of a more sustainable and just world.

9

Advocating for Change

Advocacy for change is a powerful tool in the quest for a sustainable future. It's about using one's voice, actions, and influence to effect meaningful environmental and social transformation. Advocates for change can take many forms, from individuals to community groups, non-profits, and businesses, all united by a common goal to address ecological concerns and promote sustainability.

At the individual level, change can be advocated through daily choices and behaviors. By choosing sustainable products, reducing waste, and conserving resources, individuals send a message about their values and priorities. Moreover, sharing these practices and their benefits with friends, family, and social networks can amplify their impact.

Community engagement is the next step in advocacy. Communities that come together to address local environmental issues can have a profound effect. This can involve organizing clean-up campaigns, tree planting events, or community recycling programs. Participation in local government, from attending city council meetings to voting on environmental initiatives, gives citizens a direct voice in shaping policy.

Educational outreach is another cornerstone of advocacy. Workshops, seminars, and presentations raise awareness about environmental issues and the importance of sustainability. By educating others, advocates can inspire action and foster a more informed public that's ready to support sustainable initiatives.

Non-profits and environmental organizations play a crucial role in advocating for change at a larger scale. These organizations can mobilize resources and public support to campaign for environmental policies, protect natural resources, and hold corporations and governments accountable.

Businesses also have the power to advocate for change. By adopting sustainable practices and green policies, businesses can lead by example.

They can influence their industries, supply chains, and customers, creating a ripple effect that encourages other companies to follow suit.

Advocacy for change is not without its challenges. It often requires confronting established systems and norms, pushing against resistance, and remaining resilient in the face of setbacks. However, the collective action of dedicated individuals and groups can overcome these obstacles.

Advocacy for change is multi-dimensional, encompassing a range of strategies and actions that influence policy, business practices, and public perception. From grassroots campaigns to legal challenges and policy reform, every action contributes to the broader movement for a sustainable and equitable world.

Active participation in environmental advocacy involves both speaking out and listening. Advocates must articulate the need for change and engage in dialogues that shape public opinion and policy. They serve as a bridge, connecting the scientific community, policymakers, and the public, translating complex environmental issues into actionable information.

Social media and digital platforms offer powerful tools for change advocates. They can spread messages quickly, organize movements, share success stories, and mobilize global support for environmental causes. Online petitions, awareness campaigns, and crowdfunding for green projects are examples of how digital advocacy can lead to real-world changes.

At the governmental level, advocacy means engaging with elected officials and contributing to the legislative process. Writing letters, making phone calls, or meeting with representatives can influence the development and implementation of environmental legislation. Civic engagement ensures that leaders are aware of their constituents' concerns about sustainability.

Legal advocacy is also vital in enforcing existing environmental laws and pushing for stronger regulations. Environmental lawyers and organizations often lead this charge, taking legal action to protect natural resources and hold polluters accountable.

Furthermore, fostering partnerships among businesses, non-profits, and government entities can lead to collaborative solutions that benefit the environment. These alliances can harness the strengths and resources of different sectors to address complex sustainability challenges.

Advocacy is also about resilience and long-term commitment. Change often requires sustained effort over time. Celebrating small victories along the way can provide the encouragement needed to continue striving for larger goals.

In the end, advocating for change is an expression of hope and responsibility. It's about believing in the possibility of a better future and taking the necessary steps to make that vision a reality. Each voice raised for sustainability strengthens the collective call for a greener, more just planet.

Youth engagement is increasingly recognized as a transformative force in advocating for change. Young people are not only voicing their concerns about the future but also spearheading innovative solutions and demanding action from older generations. Their involvement brings fresh perspectives and a sense of urgency to the sustainability conversation.

In the workplace, advocating for sustainable practices can take the form of green committees or corporate social responsibility initiatives. Employees can influence internal policies, advocate for energy-saving measures, or suggest company-wide sustainability training. This internal advocacy helps to shift corporate culture and can lead to significant changes in operational practices.

Education for sustainability is expanding beyond formal settings into the broader community. Public lectures, interactive exhibits, and community workshops can build a more informed citizenry. These educational efforts empower individuals with the knowledge to make more sustainable choices and to hold institutions accountable.

Consumer advocacy plays a crucial role, too. By demanding transparency and choosing to support ethical and sustainable businesses, consumers can drive market change. Conscious consumerism puts pressure on companies to prioritize sustainability, not only in their products but in their operations and supply chains as well.

Lastly, advocacy for change also means celebrating and supporting the diversity of environmental champions. From local activists to international leaders, the environmental movement is enriched by the contributions of those from all walks of life. Their collective efforts are the bedrock upon which sustainable progress is built.

The act of advocating for change is a dynamic and continuous process. It involves constant learning, adaptability, and a willingness to engage in both local actions and global movements. As each individual contributes to this tapestry of change, the movement grows stronger, weaving a resilient narrative of hope for a sustainable future.

Sustainability advocacy extends into the realm of investment and finance as well. Ethical investing strategies that exclude companies with poor environmental records and prioritize those contributing positively to the planet are reshaping the investment landscape. These strategies encourage businesses to become more sustainable to attract investors.

Community-driven change is also significant. Local initiatives like establishing community gardens, promoting the use of local products, and creating green spaces contribute to sustainable development. These projects not only enhance environmental quality but also strengthen local economies and social cohesion.

Recognition of the interdependence between humans and nature is growing, and with it, the understanding that protecting the environment is intrinsic to preserving human health and social welfare. This understanding drives advocacy that integrates environmental, health, and social policy, reflecting a holistic approach to sustainability.

Moreover, advocates for change are calling for the inclusion of sustainability in all levels of education. By embedding these principles into the curriculum, educational institutions can cultivate a generation equipped to tackle environmental challenges and lead sustainable lives.

To amplify the impact of advocacy, storytelling and the arts are employed to evoke emotional connections with environmental causes. Films, literature, music, and visual arts can convey powerful messages that inspire action and bring attention to sustainability issues.

At its core, advocating for change is about fostering a culture where sustainability is the norm. It's about creating a world where environmental considerations are woven into the fabric of everyday life, from the products we buy to the policies we support and the education we receive.

The cumulative effect of these advocacy efforts is the creation of a society deeply committed to sustainability. As this movement for change grows, it lays the groundwork for enduring environmental stewardship, ensuring that sustainability is not just a fleeting concern but a lasting commitment to our planet's future.

The momentum behind advocacy for change is bolstered by the recognition that environmental issues are inextricably linked to social justice. Advocates work to ensure that sustainability efforts address inequality and that the benefits of a green economy are shared by all, particularly those in marginalized communities who are often most affected by environmental degradation.

Corporate accountability is also a crucial focus area. Consumers and advocacy groups are increasingly holding companies to account for their environmental promises and commitments, ensuring they follow through on pledges to reduce carbon emissions, eliminate waste, or use sustainable materials.

In the political arena, advocacy takes the form of campaigning for green policies, such as subsidies for renewable energy, carbon pricing mechanisms, or legislation to curb plastic pollution. Such policies can have far-reaching effects, creating the frameworks within which individuals and companies operate and incentivizing sustainable choices.

Technology also offers new opportunities for advocacy. Digital platforms enable activists to create virtual communities that span the globe, transcending geographical boundaries to unite people around environmental causes. These platforms can also track and visualize the impact of collective actions, providing clear evidence of what can be achieved through united efforts.

The transition to a sustainable future is also about reimagining our relationship with time and progress. It's a move away from short-term gains and toward long-term sustainability, considering the legacy that will be left for future generations.

As we look toward the horizon, the role of each advocate becomes clear: to act as a custodian of the Earth, safeguarding it through thoughtful, persistent, and informed action. It's about painting a vision of the future that prioritizes the health of our planet and its inhabitants over all else.

Through the chorus of voices calling for change, through the dedicated actions of communities, and through the evolving policies and technologies, a new narrative is being written—one of resilience, responsibility, and hope. It's a narrative that celebrates our deepening connection to the environment and to each other, as we collectively journey toward a more sustainable and equitable world.

This ever-growing network of change-makers is shaping a world where sustainability isn't an afterthought but the foundation of decision-making. Grassroots movements are blossoming into widespread initiatives, influencing corporate governance and international protocols. Through this, they are demonstrating the undeniable power of collective will to create enduring change.

As the sustainable movement advances, it intersects with other critical global issues, reinforcing that our fight for environmental sustainability is also a fight for global health, for equitable access to resources, and for the protection of biodiversity. These intersections highlight the complex but interrelated challenges that our world faces and the multifaceted approach required to address them.

Environmental advocacy is becoming an integral part of cultural identity for many, a unifying element that cuts across age, geography, and background. It's a shared mission that galvanizes individuals into action, whether through lifestyle changes, community projects, or contributions to global environmental funds.

The transformation being sought is profound—renewing our societal values to align closely with ecological principles. This shift demands a paradigm change, from economies based on endless growth to ones that value sustainability and circular principles, where waste is minimized, and resources are reused.

In conclusion, the drive for sustainable change is a testament to human adaptability and resilience. It's a journey of transformation, of rethinking the ways we live, work, and interact with our environment. The dedication and passion behind advocacy for change are sowing the seeds for a healthier, more sustainable world, ensuring that future generations inherit a planet that is not only livable but flourishing.

10

〜

Future in Focus: Sustaining Momentum in Our Global Community

As we reach the final pages of our exploration into sustainable living, we turn our gaze towards the horizon, anticipating the future of sustainability shaped by emerging technologies and innovations. This future is one where sustainability is not an add-on but a foundational principle embedded in the fabric of society, powered by advancements that bring us closer to harmony with the natural world.

Emerging technologies in renewable energy, such as advanced solar photovoltaics, wind turbines that harness air currents at higher altitudes, and energy storage solutions that promise greater efficiency, are paving the way for a cleaner energy landscape. Innovations in biotechnology present breakthroughs in creating materials that are not just recyclable but biodegradable, aligning product life cycles with ecological cycles.

The future of transportation glimmers with the prospects of electric and autonomous vehicles, hyperloops, and even urban aerial mobility. These technologies aim to decrease emissions, reduce traffic congestion, and provide cleaner, more accessible transportation options.

In agriculture, the growth of precision farming and vertical farming techniques offers the possibility of higher yields with lower environmental impacts. Innovations like lab-grown meat and aquaponics are redefining sustainable food production and consumption.

Smart cities, with their integrated, data-driven approaches to energy, transport, and infrastructure, illustrate how urban living can be efficient and sustainable. The Internet of Things (IoT) and big data analytics provide the tools to optimize resource use and reduce waste.

But beyond technology, the future of sustainability is equally about people and communities. It's about the ongoing efforts of individuals who choose to live mindfully, reduce their environmental impact, and advocate for change. It's about community gardens, local clean-ups, and grassroots movements that are as much a part of the sustainability revolution as any technology.

Personal and community efforts are the lifeblood of sustainability. They demonstrate a commitment to the cause that is both heartfelt and hands-on. These efforts foster a sense of belonging and responsibility, a shared mission to protect and cherish our planet.

As we encourage these ongoing efforts, we recognize that every small action contributes to a greater good. The path to a sustainable future is a collective journey—one that we undertake as a global community, each of us playing a part in shaping the legacy we leave for the generations to come.

In closing, we acknowledge that the journey is not complete. There will always be more to learn, more to innovate, and more to do. Yet, with each step we take, we move closer to a world where living sustainably is not just an aspiration but a reality. Let this be not just the epilogue of a book but the prologue to a future where sustainability is the cornerstone of our existence.

11

Towards a Sustainable Horizon: The Collective Path Forward

In understanding our carbon footprint, we learned the significance of measuring and reducing our individual and household contributions to greenhouse gas emissions. Simple tools and lifestyle changes can significantly reduce our environmental impact.

Zero-Waste Living taught us the transformative power of the 5 Rs, highlighting how we can drastically cut down waste in our lives. From shopping habits to product choices, the zero-waste approach is both an environmental imperative and a practical lifestyle.

Sustainable Fashion uncovered the hidden costs of our clothing. We discovered the benefits of choosing sustainable brands, caring for clothes to extend their longevity, and participating in clothing swaps, which collectively forge a path toward a more ethical and environmentally friendly fashion industry.

Green Building and Sustainable Home Management opened our eyes to the potential of our living spaces to contribute to sustainability. Energy-efficient designs, renewable energy, and water-saving practices turn homes into eco-friendly havens.

Renewable Energy Solutions showed us the promising frontier of clean energy. From solar to wind, and from hydro to geothermal, we saw a future energized by renewable sources that lessen our dependency on fossil fuels and reduce pollution.

Sustainable Transportation illustrated the importance of rethinking how we move. Adopting public transit, cycling, walking, and electric vehicles can lead to cleaner air and less congested, more livable cities.

Responsible Consumption and Recycling emphasized the critical role of making informed choices and the positive impact of recycling right.

From mindful purchasing to proper sorting, our actions can lead to significant environmental benefits.

Advocating for Change inspired us to use our voices and actions to drive environmental progress. We learned that by engaging in advocacy and education, we could influence policy, support sustainable business practices, and encourage others to live more sustainably.

In conclusion, the collective impact of individual and community actions is profound. Each sustainable choice, each advocacy effort, and each educational endeavor contributes to the global tapestry of sustainability. When we change our daily habits, we not only improve our own lives but also support the health of our planet and society at large. This book has not only offered insights and strategies but also a call to action—to live responsibly, to consume thoughtfully, and to protect and cherish our shared home for present and future generations.

12

Appendices

A. Glossary of Terms

The glossary serves as an essential tool for readers to demystify jargon and technical terms encountered throughout the book. This comprehensive list includes definitions for terms such as:

- **Carbon Footprint**: The total amount of greenhouse gases, including carbon dioxide and methane, that are emitted by an individual, event, organization, service, or product.
- **Composting**: A natural process of recycling organic matter, such as leaves and food scraps, into a valuable fertilizer that can enrich soil and plants.
- **Sustainable Development**: Development that meets the needs of the present without compromising the ability of future generations to meet their own needs.

B. Directory of Resources

This directory provides a vetted list of resources, making it easier for readers to continue their education and apply the principles of sustainability in their lives. The resources include:

- **Websites:**

  - Environmental Protection Agency (EPA): For guidelines on various environmental initiatives and statistics.
  - Greenpeace: For updates on global campaigns and how to get involved.
  - The Sustainable Development Goals (SDGs) by the UN: For understanding the global targets set for sustainability.

- **Apps:**

  - Good On You: For checking the ethical and sustainability credentials of clothing brands.
  - JouleBug: For turning sustainable living into a fun and competitive game.
  - Ecosia: A search engine that plants trees with its ad revenue.

- **Books:**

  - "Silent Spring" by Rachel Carson: The book that spearheaded the environmental movement by exposing the dangers of pesticides.
  - "This Changes Everything" by Naomi Klein: A book discussing capitalism vs. the climate.
  - "Cradle to Cradle" by William McDonough & Michael Braungart: A seminal text on designing products with the full lifecycle in mind.

C. List of Influential Environmental Organizations

Connecting with organizations can turn awareness into action. Here are a few:

- **World Wildlife Fund (WWF)**: Known for its efforts in wildlife conservation and endangered species.
- **Sierra Club**: One of the oldest environmental organizations in the US, involved in promoting clean energy and conservation.
- **350.org**: An international movement aimed at ending the use of fossil fuels and transitioning to renewable energy.

Each organization offers unique ways to get involved, from local projects and advocacy to global initiatives. Whether it's through volunteering, education, or donations, these groups provide avenues for active participation in the sustainability movement.

The appendices of this book are more than just a reference; they're an invitation to continue exploring, learning, and engaging with the world of sustainability. They provide the tools and connections to not only understand the material but to become an active participant in the ongoing dialogue and efforts for a sustainable future.